The Tale
of Little Bevan

by
Robert Alan Evans

A co-commission with
Creative Arts East

The Tale of Little Bevan
was commissioned by Pentabus and Creative Arts East.
It was first performed at Pentabus Theatre, Bromfield,
Shropshire, on Wednesday 16 October 2019.

The Tale of Little Bevan

By Robert Alan Evans

Cast

Owen Aaronovitch
Annie Grace
Andy Peppiette

Creative Team

Director	**Sophie Motley**
Designer	**Alyson Cummins**
Lighting Designer	**James Mackenzie**
Composer & Musical Director	**Little John Nee**
Movement Director	**Vicki Igbokwe**
Voice & Accent Coach	**Emma Stevens-Johnson**
Production Manager	**Tom Richmond**
Touring Stage Manager	**Sophie Spillane**

Special thanks to

Artists & Engineers, Clean Break, Sarah Dickenson,
John Dollimore, Sophie Ellerby, Ingrid Fairman, Jill Golzen,
Annie Grace, Jane Leitch, Ben Lewis, Laura Lomas,
Bev Mirza, Will O'Connell, Maggie, Graham and Lola Playford,
Christine Reilly, Zara Ramm, Amelia Sears,
Sherman Theatre, Tracey Woolley, Wortwell Bell.

Tour Dates

16 October | Pentabus Theatre | Shropshire
17 October | Pentabus Theatre | Shropshire
18 October | All Stretton Village Hall | Shropshire
19 October | Quatt Village Hall | Shropshire

22 October | The Courtyard, Hereford | Herefordshire
25 October | Edgton Village Hall with Lydbury North | Shropshire
26 October | Culmington Village Hall | Shropshire
27 October | Clun Memorial Hall | Shropshire

29 October | Ketteringham Village Hall | Norfolk
30 October | Wortwell Community Centre | Norfolk
31 October | Westacre Theatre | Norfolk

07 November | Barnacle Village Hall | Warwickshire
08 November | Spring Arts Centre | Derbyshire
09 November | Great Longstone Village Hall | Derbyshire
10 November | Bishampton Village Hall | Worcestershire

13 November | Kingston on Soar Village Hall | Nottinghamshire
14 November | Ropsley Village Hall | Worcestershire
15 November | Ombersley Memorial Hall | Worcestershire
16 November | Allington Village Hall | Lincolnshire
17 November | Dunston Village Hall | Lincolnshire

20 November | Salisbury Playhouse | Dorset
22 November | Halstock Village Hall | Dorset
23 November | Briantspuddle Village Hall | Dorset
24 November | Child Okeford Village Hall | Dorset

27 November | The Market Theatre, Ledbury | Herefordshire
28 November | Vowchurch & Turnastone Village Hall | Herefordshire
29 November | Clive Hall, Moreton Say | Shropshire
30 November | Ludlow Assembly Rooms | Shropshire

Cast

OWEN AARONOVITCH | Tony

Theatre includes: *Treasure Island* (New Vic); *Flatspin, Gameplan, This Happy Breed* (Pitlochry Festival Theatre); *Crackers, Dream Topping* (Belgrade Theatre); *Casualties, Killing Camilla* (Mad Dogs Theatre Company); *Breaking the Silence* (Nottingham Playhouse); *Moby Dick* (Compass Theatre); *Pinocchio, Robin Hood* (Gardner Arts Centre); *Dick Whittington* (New Elgiva Theatre); *The Ladykillers* (UK tour); *Aladdin* (Stafford Gatehouse); *The Great Gatsby* (American Drama Group); *Red Dust, Blue Dreams* (Public Parts); *The Grapes of Wrath, Nobody's Children, A View from the Bridge* (Sheffield Crucible); *The Waltz* (West Yorkshire Playhouse); *Cyril Preston, The Hunchback of Notre Dame, The Plough and the Stars* (New Vic Theatre); *The Secret Agent* (Dr Fosters Theatre Company); *The Murder of Sherlock Holmes* (TNT Theatre); *Dr Sullivan and Mr Gilbert* (Mull Little Theatre).

Television includes: *The Tudors, Doctors, Court Room, Holby City, Coronation Street, Alarmed, Heartbeat, Emmerdale, Strange But True, The Bill, Cracker, Medics, Out of Sight, A Touch of Frost*.

ANNIE GRACE | Gill

Theatre and opera credits include: *The Last Ship* (UK and Canadian tours); *The Winter's Tale* (Royal Lyceum Edinburgh); *Tir Na Nog, Hysteria* (Òran Mór); *Threads* (Stellar Quines); *Dark Woods, Deep Snow, The Bloody Great Big Border Ballad* (Northern Stage); *The Strange Undoing of Prudencia Hart, The Tin Forest, Blabbermouth, The Great, Yes, No, Don't Know Five Minute Theatre Show, Peter Pan* (National Theatre of Scotland); *Ane Satyre of the Thrie Estaitis* (A&BC Theatre); *Little Bit of Northern Light* (Scottish Opera).

ANDY PEPPIETTE | Mikey

Andy trained at Rose Bruford College of Theatre and Performance.

Theatre includes: *Mancub* (Cumbernauld Theatre); *Blowing Your Paradise Away* (Edinburgh Fringe Festival/Lump's Room); *The Medium* (Magnetic Opera); *Britain Ltd* (Ad Infinitum); *The Lost Boy* (Catherine Wheels).

Film includes: *Varken* (Sartorious Productions).

Creative Team

ROBERT ALAN EVANS | Writer

Robert is a writer, director and deviser working across the UK.

Theatre includes: *The Woods*, *A Girl in a Car with a Man* (Royal Court); *Kes* (Leeds Playhouse and Catherine Wheels); *The River and the Mountain* (LAMDA); *Peter Pan*, *The Sleeping Beauties* (Sherman Cymru); *Ignition* (National Theatre of Scotland); *Mikey and Addie* (2012 Cultural Olympiad); *The Voice Thief* – winner of Critics' Awards for Theatre in Scotland; *Caged, Pobby and Dingan* – winner of TMA Award for Best Show for Children and Young People, *Pondlife* – winner of the Prix d'Orpheon, *Kappa* (Catherine Wheels); *Pinocchio* (Northampton Theatre Royal); *Mr Snow*, *The Night Before Christmas* (Leeds Playhouse).

As director: *The Dig* (Paul Curley); *Crumble's Search for Christmas* (Leeds Playhouse); *Mr Snow* (MacRobert Arts Centre); *Aruba*, *Fish Story* (People Can Run); *Naked Neighbour Twitching Blind* (Tramway).

Dance includes: *The Beginners Guide to Flying*, *Little Red*, *TigerTale* (Barrowland Ballet/Tramway).

Radio includes: The Cracks.

SOPHIE MOTLEY | Director

Sophie grew up in South Shropshire and was based in Ireland from 2002 to 2016. She has directed five productions as Artistic Director of Pentabus: *Crossings*, *Festival!*, *Here I Belong*, *Wolves Are Coming for You* and *New Futures*. Previously she was co-artistic director of WillFredd Theatre, Associate Director of Rough Magic in Dublin, Staff Director at English National Opera and Resident Assistant Director at the Abbey Theatre, Ireland's national theatre.

ALYSON CUMMINS | Designer

Theatre and opera include: *Last Orders at the Dockside, Heartbreak House, The Risen People, Quietly, Perve, No Escape* (Abbey Theatre Dublin); *L'Arlesiana, Zazà, Così Fan Tutte* (Opera Holland Park); *Iolanta, L'Enfant et les Sortilèges* (Royal Academy of Music); *Thick as Thieves* (Clean Break and Theatr Clwyd); *The Lion in Winter* (English Theatre Frankfurt); *Tosca* (Icelandic Opera); *Gulliver's Travels* (YMT/ Lyric Belfast); *Sinners, Pentecost* – Best Set Design, Irish Times Theatre Award 2015, *Mixed Marriage, The Nativity & The Gingerbread Mix-Up* (Lyric Belfast); *Jacques Brel Is Alive and Well and Living In Paris* (Gate Theatre Dublin); *The Nest* (Young Vic/Lyric Belfast); *Quietly* (Abbey Theatre/Irish Rep /Public Theater); *Fabric* – Edinburgh Fringe First (Robin Rayner); *Macbeth* (Iford Arts); *This Lime Tree Bower* (Eoin Kilkenny); *The Lighthouse* (Royal Opera House, Linbury Studio); *The Night Alive* (DTF/Lyric Belfast); *Be Infants in Evil* (Druid); *Summertime* (Tinderbox); *Before It Rains* (Bristol Old Vic and Sherman Cymru); *Pornography* (Waking Exploits); *Pigeon* (Carpet Theatre); *Ruben Guthrie* (Iron Bark); *How the World Began (*Arcola theatre); *Hamlet* (Second Age); *The Trailer of Bridget Dinnigan* (ITM); *Colleen Bawn* (Project/Civic/Bedrock); *Off Plan* (RAW); *Serious Money, Dying City* (Rough Magic Seeds); *The Trials of Brother Jero* (Samuel Beckett Theatre); *Through a Film Darkly* (Arambe); *Ya Get Me* (The Old Vic).

Alyson studied Architecture at University College Dublin and trained at Motley. She was a finalist in the Linbury Biennial Prize for stage design in 2007.

JAMES MACKENZIE | Lighting Designer

For Pentabus: *As the Crow Flies, Milked, This Land.*

Recent theatre and dance credits include: *Handbagged* (Salisbury Playhouse); *Hansel and Gretel* (Uchenna Dance/The Place); *This is an Island* (Gary Clarke/Dancexchange); *Hansel* (Salisbury Playhouse); *Run* (2Faced Dance); *Dark Wood, Deep Snow* (Northern Stage); *Ten* (Tavaziva Dance); *Jason and the Argonauts, Macbeth* (Courtyard Theatre); *Close Distance* (Parlor Dance); *Finding Joy* (Vamos Theatre); *Rock, Suitcase Story* (Dance East); *The Legend of Captain Crow's Teeth* (Unicorn Theatre); *DNA* (Hull Truck); *Herding Cats* (Hampstead); *See* (Company Decalage); *Shattered* (Feral Productions); *Steam* (Royal Festival Hall); *Cut it Out* (Young Vic); *Speaking on Tongues* (Birmingham School of Acting). James is also the Director of the award-winning ZOO Venues at the Edinburgh Festival Fringe. He trained at Rose Bruford College.

LITTLE JOHN NEE | Composer and Musical Director

Little John Nee is a playwright, performer and musician based in the west of Ireland. He is a recipient of an Irish Times Theatre Award for Sound Design, a Helen Hayes Award Nominee, a Prix Italia Special Mention Award, and in 2016 was elected to Aosdána, which honours artists whose work has made an outstanding contribution to the creative arts in Ireland.

VICKI IGBOKWE | Movement Director

Dance and theatre credits include, as director/choreographer: *Our Mighty Groove*, *The Head Wrap Diaries*, *Hansel and Gretel* (UK tours for Uchenna Dance); *The Head Wrap Diaries: Fierce and Free* (Sadler's Wells and The Lowry). As associate director and choreographer: *Provok'd* (Guildhall School of Music and Drama). As movement director: *The Woods* (Royal Court); *Princess and the Hustler* (Eclipse Theatre, Bristol Old Vic and Hull Truck Theatre). As movement director and choreographer: *Red Dust Road* (National Theatre of Scotland and HOME Manchester); *Mid Life* (Diverse City); *Seven Ages of Patience* (Kiln Theatre). As mass movement choreographer: London 2012 Olympic and Paralympic opening and closing ceremonies; Sochi 2014 Olympic and Paralympic opening and closing ceremonies; Glasgow 2014 Commonwealth Games opening ceremony; 2017 Islamic Solidarity Games opening and closing ceremonies.

EMMA STEVENS-JOHNSON | Voice & Accent Coach

For Pentabus: *Crossings*, *Here I Belong*.

Emma has worked within film and theatre for over twenty years. She began teaching accents in London in 2002, and has worked on international productions such as *The Trial of Christine Keeler* and *Hellboy*; the critically acclaimed film *Submarine*; the Netflix series *Apostle* and *15 Days* for Channel 5; *Requiem* and *Ordinary Lies* for the BBC. She has worked for BBC Cymru, S4C, BBC Radio and is Voice Coach in Residence for Theatre Na n'Og. She has also worked for Theatre Royal Bath, Wales Millennium Theatre Company, Waking Exploits and Hijinx. Emma is a lecturer in Voice at the Royal Welsh College of Music and Drama. She has a Masters in Vocal Studies from Central School of Speech and Drama.

PENTABUS

Pentabus is the nation's rural theatre company. We are the only professional theatre company in the UK whose vision is singularly rural. We tour new plays about the contemporary rural world to new audiences in village halls, fields, festivals and theatres, telling stories with local relevance and national impact. We believe that every person living in an isolated rural community has a right to exceptional theatre. We are based on a farm in Shropshire, and to date all of our work has been made here. It then tours village halls and theatres locally and nationally. Over four and a half decades we've produced 171 new plays, reached over half a million audience members, won a prestigious South Bank Show award, a Fringe First and were the first to live stream from a village hall. We have hosted a writer in residence since 2014 and they have gone on to be commissioned by the Royal Court, Birmingham Rep, Royal Welsh College, the Bush, Nottingham Playhouse and HighTide.

We are a champion for rural young people aged sixteen to twenty-five. Pentabus Young Company is our new initiative offering workshops, master classes, work experience and mentorships, as well as the opportunity to join our Young Writers' Group, which has been running for six years. Previous participants of the Young Writers' Group have had their work presented at Ludlow Fringe, Latitude Festival and Hereford Courtyard. It is a springboard into further study and the arts industry, with over 50 per cent of our Young Writers going on to be published and professional writers.

You can find out more about us at
www.pentabus.co.uk

Twitter: @pentabustheatre | Facebook: Pentabus Theatre
Instagram: Pentabustheatrecompany

Pentabus Theatre Company,
Bromfield, Ludlow, Shropshire, SY8 2JU

Pentabus is a registered charity (Number 287909).
We rely on the generosity of our donors, small and large,
to help us to continue to make world-class theatre.
We would like to thank all our supporters including:

Torchbearers
Madeleine Bedford, Richard Burbidge, Anne Haydock,
Camilla Harrison, Diane Lennan, Joseph Motley, Jenny Pearce,
Michael Penn, Ros Robins, Hermoine Salwey, Neil Stuttard,
Barbara Ann Tweedie, Mary Wells

Ragleth/Beacons
James Mayor, Cecilia Motley, Chaz Webb

Pentabus' Business Supporters
Bayfield Van Hire, Britpart, Continental Fireplaces,
Craven Design and Print, Morris Property, Robinsons Ciders,
Tanners, The Insurance Network.

Pentabus is also supported by the Clive & Sylvia Richards Charity,
the Haystack Trust, The Leche Trust and The Millichope Foundation.

The Tale of Little Bevan

Robert Alan Evans is a writer, director and deviser. He has written extensively for young people and co-created several dance pieces. Theatre includes *The Woods*, *A Girl in a Car with a Man*, *Aruba*, *The Voice Thief*, *Caged*, *Pondlife*, *Mikey and Addie*, *Kappa* and *The River and the Mountain*. His adaptations include *Kes*, *Peter Pan*, *Pinocchio*, *Pobby and Dingan* and *The Sleeping Beauties*. His collaboration with choreographers include *Tiger, Tiger Tale* and *Little Red*. He grew up outside Cardiff and has lived and worked in Edinburgh, Glasgow and now London.

ROBERT ALAN EVANS

The Tale of Little Bevan

FABER & FABER

First published in 2019
by Faber and Faber Limited
74–77 Great Russell Street, London WC1B 3DA

Typeset by Country Setting, Kingsdown, Kent CT14 8ES
Printed in England by CPI Group (UK) Ltd, Croydon, Surrey CRO 44Y

A CIP record for this book is available from the British Library

ISBN 978-0-571-36086-4

2 4 6 8 10 9 7 5 3 1

The Tale of Little Bevan was first performed at Pentabus Theatre, Bromfield, Shropshire, on 16 October 2019, prior to a national tour. The cast, in alphabetical order, was as follows:

Owen Aaronovitch
Annie Grace
Andy Peppiette

Director Sophie Motley
Designer Alyson Cummins
Lighting Designer James Mackenzie
Songs by Little John Nee
Lyrics by Little John Nee and Robert Alan Evans
Composer and Musical Director Little John Nee
Movement Director Vicki Igbokwe
Voice and Accent Coach Emma Stevens-Johnson

Thanks to Laura Lomas for giving up
her weekend for me as I descended into that
very special tunnel reserved for lost writers.
Also to Ben Lewis and Amelia Sears
who provided some light at the end.

Characters

Tony
Mikey
Gill
Josie
Pat
Driver
Date
Andy
Mrs Hargreaves
Mrs MacKenzie

THE TALE OF LITTLE BEVAN

ONE

A long, long time ago.
    A hand is sinking into the ground.
    We hear holy music.

This story begins with St Agathus.
Such a very long time ago that even the words we need
    had not yet arrived.
Though they were about to.
Harvest moon, eight hundred and sixty-five. As
    Christians fled from the vast heathen army that had
    come from across the sea.
About to smash down upon the Kingdom of the Angles.

Drit, dregg, myki, myre.
They will set this world on fire.
Pillage. Rape. Kill. Burn.
Hope must be hidden.

And so, with nowhere to go,
It was below that Agathus fled.

In North Folks' earth; the dirt, the muck, the myre.
Where heathen's fire could not find her.
Went the holy lady of the Fens.
To return again, when she is most needed.

    The hand disappears below.

TWO

Tony has been staring at a piece of blank paper.
    He rips it up in frustration and even eats some of the
pieces.
    Which he realises are disgusting, so he tries to drink
some water in an old glass.
    Which he realises is also disgusting and spits out.

Tony.

Tony Come on! Come on!

Trying for the two hundred and sixteenth time to start
    his book.

Tony who only seven years before was so much more.
A colossus.
A god.
A man who was once very close to being made a semi-
    permanent member of the University of East Anglia's
    History Department.
For his work on the origins and myths of ninth-century
    East Anglia.
With specific reference to the cult of St Agathus.

Oooooooh it was good stuff.
His last article in which he had come close to proving
    where Agathus' remains might lie had been called . . .

'Almost too hot to handle'

and

'Very well researched'

and

'Interesting'.

A man on the up.

Until . . .

We hear a phone ring, distantly.
  The sound of Tony's mum on the other end, in
distress.

'Tony . . .
Love.'

That day. Seven years before.
When Tony's career hit a wall.
His mum had had a fall.

And so began the next six years of his life.
You care, and then you don't.
Float further from the world; your colleagues,
    the teaching.
Until eventually you stop going in.
They try to call, but it's all . . .
The sound of his mother at night watching telly.
Him trying to write, still trying to be somebody. Until
    eventually . . .
He gives in. Watches Mel and Sue as they talk about
    a master bake.

Tony It's cake, Mum.
Cake!
We just need to get you up.
On here.
Your son. I'm your son.
Just lift this one.
This one.
No.
This one.
(*Suddenly snapping.*)
THIS ONE! THIS ONE! THIS ONE!

Silence.
Gone.

Now he could finally get on.

Back to his book.

He'd done his research. Read almost every book.
Though he felt there might be a few notes to make
    on St Agathus' crook. Which some believed might
    have been a sword. Others a stick. Tony felt he needed
    to really understand every angle before he could even
    dream of putting pen to paper.
Then he'd spent two months trying to get the title right.
He'd toyed with something minimal like just a Celtic
    symbol.

Nah. Too 'in-the-know', elite.

He wanted his book to appeal to the man on the street.

Tony 'Agathus: Woman or God'.

Crossed it out in a hurry.
Thinking it sounded a bit . . . Jenni Murray.

Tony Yes. Yes. It's coming. It's coming.
It's practical, informative, yet has a certain spice.

'The Historical Origins and Details of the Figure Known
    as St Agathus: Her Relationship to Pre-Christian
    Ritual and the Kingdom of the East Angles . . . with
    Dates, Maps and a Study of the Derivation of Related
    Norfolkshire Place Names . . . Along with a
    Comprehensive and Fully Illustrated Guide to the
    Appearance or Non-appearance of St Agathus in the
    Stained Glass Art of the Area . . .'

*Tony crumples up the paper in frustration. He lets out
a sort of desperate moan, trying to hold everything in.
He's like a wounded animal.*

How was he meant to write when –
There.

That.
A gap.
On the shelves.
His mum's statue. Gone.
How?
She must've taken it.
That . . . cow!

Tony's sister had come a few days before.
'Are you okay?'
But really to start a sort of war of attrition.
Wanted 'a few of Mum's things.
Something to remember her by.'
But why? Why should she have a thing?
Where was she for the washing, the cleaning, the muck
    and the mire?

Tony had smiled.
Given her a box.

Tony Here, fill this.
Put it in the shed.
That way you can come get it if I'm out, or in bed.
I'll be changing the locks.
Some of the carers that came . . .
Very nice, but I don't quite trust them all the same.

'But you'll give me a key.'

Tony . . . Of course.

He'd followed her round. See what she took.
The odd photo. A book of recipes.
Fine.
But the statue.

Tony That's mine.

'I thought Mum left it to me.'

Tony No. No. Well, we'll see.

She must've come back and swiped it.

A gap on the shelf. Rage.
Better than uncertainty. Than staring at a blank page.
Wondering how the hell you'll ever get a job at your age.
No!

THREE

We see Mikey. He is hunched over his phone.

Mikey.

Mikey (*under his breath, staring at the phone*) Come on!
Come on!

If you'd been watching, say twenty minutes before.
You'd have seen Mikey vault over Tony's wall and
enter his shed.

A Grindr message sound. *

— *Hey!*

Yes! *Hey. Sorry bout that.*
Got cut off.

— *Yeah, thought you'd left me there, mate.*

No! I mean – (*Deleting and retyping.*) *Yeah, sorry.*

— *What you doing?*

Eh . . .
Reading.
No one says reading. No one's reading. No one reads.

— *Like an actual book? With sentences?*

Yeah. Haha.

Gone. Gone. Lost him.

---

* Grindr is a geo-social dating application for gay, bi, queer and
trans people. It has a very specific message sound.

— *Nice. What is it?*

It *was* pretty cool. 1984.

— *I love that one. Feels like we're living it.*

Yeah. My mum's like the thought police.

— (*Laughing tears emoji.*)

He gets my jokes.

— *How old you?*

Should he come clean?

. . .
Nah.
Eighteen.

— *Cool. You're hot btw. Where's the pic from?*

. . .
Argentina.

And he's back.
And the chat.
Never been like this before.
An actual person. Funny and sweet and . . .

— *So, do you wanna meet?*

Shit.

Tony Something not right.
In the sunny September light, Tony can see in the shed.
A sort of glow.
Then gone.

How about next week?

— *Have to be tonight. I'm off to uni on Monday.*
Nervous.

(*Mouthing to the phone.*) I love you.

Okay.

— You got wheels?

Yeah. Two . . . that would do.

— Town?

There's a nice pub. Called The Bell. In Wortwell.

— What time?

Nine?

— See you there.

Tony What the hell are you doing?

Mikey Shit.
Tony.

What was he doing, crouched on the floor? Sweaty paw
   hiding his phone.
Alone.
Oh . . .

Tony Michael. Were you . . . ?

Mikey No.
Get up. Just get away.

Tony Because I know it's hard for young people today
   with . . . well, with the pressures of . . . the body.

Oh God.

Mikey No. Really, Mr Grieves, I just needed –
Your internet.

Tony What?

Mikey My mum . . . sometimes she forgets to pay the bill.
And you know they turned the mast off on the hill.
So . . . I hook on to yours sometimes.
Actually you should probably change your password.

Not that it's wrong, but 'password' itself, it's just not
    that strong.
. . .
I suppose I should . . .

Scrabbles to get up.
And that's when Tony sees on the shelf above.
A cardboard box.
And peeking out the statue he'd always loved. His
    mother's Virgin and Child.
Almost in slow mo. Tony can see what's about to happen.
The boy not right. Something gone.

Dead leg.

Reaches out to hang on to something.
Grabs the shelf which due to maybe not being the best
    DIY job in the world.
Pivots. The box and statue hurled.
Mary, flying headlong, hits the roof.
Which might've been proof of a God as she stayed intact.
But then in fact ricocheted off, hit a wall and smashed
    to pieces after all.

Silence.

The sound of nothing really.

Actually there was the sound of a goose flying over.

Back when he was ten, Tony once came down to find his
    mum sitting in her favourite chair. Talking to the air.
    The statue in hand. A song. Was it a song she sang?

We hear music of St Agathus.

He'd watched this woman, strange to him somehow.
Was it even his mum?
He's lost.

Tony I'm lost, Mum.

Mikey Mr Grieves, I'm sorry.

Tony Get out!
Now!

In the silence Tony feels this sort of . . .
Well, something like a darkness start to rise. Start to
    choke . . .

And then he spies. There. On the floor.

He picks up a parchment.

Had it been there before?
No. Old. Had been hidden in the statue.

And something goes off in Tony's head.
This sort of tinkling bell far away. The sort of sound
    that dreams are made of.
Because this is the sort of thing, Tony knows, that
happens at the start of *Indiana Jones*.

FOUR

Across the village. Fly! Come on! Come on!
We haven't introduced everyone.

FIVE

Five p.m.
Gill.
Standing still.
Bedroom. Calm. Listens, nothing, just the tick of the
    alarm clock, next to Rob's book. He was reading
    about the nesting habits of bats.
She'd always loved that. This village. The peace.
The geese flying over head. That time of year. Departure.

Everything was ready, pretty much.
Downstairs, enough food to kill, if it all landed on top
   of you at once.
Village favourites. Gill's famous 'Cassoulet Rustique'.
   A sort of chic sausage affair.
Then there were salads and salmon, a whole tray of
   dressed crab. She liked to educate people's palates,
   nothing drab.
The things she'd made every year for her Harvest Moon
   Ball.
And to top it all, her punch.
The thirtieth year.
There'd been ups and downs, the time they set the thatch
   on fire. The time Pat got her head stuck in the
   tombola. The year Andy lost a molar after someone
   had accidentally left their baking beans in the quiche.
Oops!
But Gill felt that overall it . . . well, it had been a ball.
A good party. Hadn't it?

Downstairs a knock at the door.

Gill Josie, hi.

Josie Gill. Sorry, can't stop. I just wanted to pop over
   and say I'm really sorry, but me and Steve can't come
   tonight.

Gill What?
You have to.

Josie There's been a cancellation at the Three Musketeers.
We've been on the list almost a year.
And you know Steve and his Michelin stars.
Getting a table's like a mission to Mars.
Very small window of opportunity, he says.
So you see . . .
Sorry.

Gill Right. Yes. No problem.

Josie How are things?

Gill Things? Things are great.

Josie Only, it's funny, but Steve was in Norwich today. And guess who was there?

A sudden tightness inside. Hide it. Hide.

Josie Rob.

Gill Really?

Josie And, well, I just remember you said he was away on a job.

Gill He is. He was. He's back.

Josie I see, because Steven said he asked something quite funny. He said 'How's Gill?'

Gill He's such a silly.

Josie And I thought . . .

Gill What?
He got back last night.

Josie Right.

Gill Long flight.
In fact I should really go and . . .

Josie Okay.

Inside. The glint of the glasses laid out.
Loads the dishwasher, turns it on.
Then stands for a while looking out the window. To the woods at the back. Imagines herself in there. Running full pelt like she's in some kind of horror. She likes to do that sometimes. Would never tell a soul. She imagines what it's like to be chased by, what? A man

with a knife? No, too much. She doesn't care what's
behind, she just likes to think about the branches
underfoot. Clothes ripped and torn. Face pale. She
stops and holds on to a tree. Looks down to the cottage,
the life she once had, into the kitchen warm and cosy.
Remembers what it was like to order the white goods
from John Lewis. Miele. The carpets and the suite.
Remembers what it was like to have the wet room
put in. The multifuel stove. Was a wreck when they
bought it. Her and Rob. Now look at it. Perfect.

Whatever's chasing is getting close.
She looks to the woods. Runs further in.

Gill Hello? Yes. Is that the Three Musketeers?
I'd like to cancel a booking . . . .
Tonight.
Wright. Steve and Josie Wright.

Harvest Moon. She'd always liked to think of the
village enjoying the fruits of the year.
Tonight though would be different.
This year, bitter fruit had grown.
Tonight they would reap what they had sown.

SIX

What do you wear?
Jeans, T-shirt. Hair. Hair.
Smell. Should I wax?
Wax what?
Oh God.
Shave? Shave it off?
Is it so obvious? Bumfluff.
Pout. Frown. Butch. Lay down and go to sleep.
NO!
Time! Time please ladies.

Teeth. (*As he cleans his teeth.*) Sticks his head out of the
　　Velux and looks at the dying afternoon. The moon
　　pale, a smudge starting to rise. The blue to darker blue
　　of vast Norfolk skies. For the first time in a while he
　　feels the space of this land. The stretch. The span. Been
　　here forever.
Five forty-five.
Okay. Time to kill. The Bell about a two-hour cycle.
Far enough away so he wouldn't bump into anyone.
Will they serve him? Shit.

'Pint of . . .'
'Lager.'
'Lager.'
'Pint of lager, please.'
'Hi.' 'Hey.' 'Hey.'

　　Imagines meeting the guy.

'Yeah.'
'Thanks. You too.'

Oh God. Oh God oh God oh God oh God.

　　He gets really panicked.

Calm. It's fine.
(*Looking at his phone.*) Re-reads every line.
Calms him. He's funny.
Mikey looks at his own profile pic.
A man called Nick.
From a blog Mike had found on the internet.
Tanned. Standing on a mountain. Smiling.
And then more; hiking, sky-diving. He was travelling the
　　world in a camper van. And every photo, every update
　　was . . . it made Mikey hurt, or ache, or something
　　like that. This perfect life being lived. When his was
　　so . . . small.
And . . . he hadn't meant to, but just to see. He'd used it.

'Got any pics?'

'Yeah. This is me'.

And the response. My God! This is what it was to be
    loved.

The sound of Grindr messages coming through.

Over and over.

To look like that. To be him.

And now a date.

He should send a picture.

The real him. So he knows.

Pose.

He takes a photo. Looks at it.

Skinny little shit.

Can't even look at it.

Delete. Delete it all.

Six o'clock. That'll do.

Should he leave a note for his mum?

Split shift, she wouldn't be back till two or three.

He puts out all the things to make a cup of tea, so she'd
    know he'd thought of her.

Mug, tea-bag, fills the kettle just right. He could do it
    later, be back way before her.

But somehow it calms him to think of her now.

Always has.

Wishes he could tell her. A knot he's carried round for
    so long.

The time when he was twelve and sat on the stairs,
    daring himself.

Just do it.

Just do it.

She wouldn't even care.

But the knot would rise and wrap round his neck. Slowly
    tighten, till he was choking with it. And all he could

do was crawl up to bed. Another night where he
hadn't said. Anything.

SEVEN

Six-fifteen and Mikey can be seen cycling off out of the
    village.
Hey, Pat.
Hi, Mikey. Not going to the party?
Maybe later.
Nice boy. Shame there's no one else his age.
Pat off to post a letter. The phone box was gone, but
    they'd left them this one thing. The postbox.
And the notice board. Pat always liked to take a look.
    Even though it hadn't changed from yesterday.
She'd re-read everything.

THE VILLAGE NOTICE-BOARD SONG

One the first of September, yoga resumes
At the back of the hall in the old snooker rooms
Remember to bring your own mat
Weight-watchers for seniors
Eat healthier dinners
There's no need to diet
We help you get thinner
Time to get rid of that fat

Everything you need to know
On the village noticeboard

Car-boot fundraiser
For a defibrillator
Please spread the word
Tell friends and neighbours
Friday in the cricket ground
Holistic bee-keeping

Homeopathy for pets
Natural healing
Recommended by vets
Six classes for thirty-five pounds

Everything you need to know
On the village notice board

Landscapes by Andy, decking and patios
No job too small. No job too grandiose
Idiots guide to the personal computer
Classes with Steve, accredited tutor
That's an interesting font
For a Michelin star restaurant

Everything you need to know
On the village notice board

But Pat's car is still for sale
Since her eyesight started to fail
Her son said it wasn't safe
She drove the wrong way on the motorway
Pat's car's still for sale.

One last chore and Pat could go get ready.

EIGHT

The sound of a church door closing.
   Tony jumps.

Half past six.
Tony standing waiting. His pupils dilating as he adjusts
   to the sudden hushed dark.
All clear. He was alone.
And looking for what . . . ?

It had happened like this.
After the shed, the statue, the smashing to bits. Tony
   had taken his find.

Carefully unfolded.
Lo and beholded.

> *The music of St Agathus. We see him unfold the*
> *parchment. It is like a light shines out at him.*
> *Tony reads, roughly translating on the fly.*

Something something. 'Agathus, daughter of Anna.
    Protector of . . . lonely.
Below North Folk's earth, uncorrupted she lies.
Come to her through the church of the open skies.'

The rest a blur. But it didn't matter.
He was going to secure his name in the early medieval
    historians' hall of fame.
Which admittedly didn't have that many people in it.
    But still . . .
Because Tony was one of very few people who knew that
    the church of the open skies was what they once called
    Little Bevan's very own St Peter and St Paul's.

> *There is a sound. He jumps. It echoes in the church.*

Is she somewhere here? Agathus.
Buried below.
No. That doesn't feel right.

What would Indiana Jones do?
Tries to think back to the films, one and two.
He'd have found a crystal, something along those lines.
So when the sun shines in the east window a beam of
    light would fall from heaven, on to a map of Little
    Bevan and reveal in a moment of total glory where
    Agathus was buried, end of story.

Tony sits.
No beams shone.
Just the sound of Andy's mower far away. He'd bought
    a sit-on.

Two pews up. Cut out for him in time and space. His
    mum's place.
Where she sat every Sunday.

Came here almost to the end.
Spat on him the day he said he could no longer take her.
His back knackered, and her so weak it would break her.
The vicar came, but it wasn't the same.
Some kind of shame, she felt. For what was happening
    to her.
Godless man. Cruel son.
Pull yourself together.
Breathing heavy now.

He goes and sits where she once did. And it's true that at
    that moment the sun slid in through the window at the
    end.
Jesus illuminated. Nice smile. Tony leans back for a
    moment. Lets himself go. For the first time in . . .

We feel the presence of Agathus.
    Tony has nearly nodded off.
    He suddenly sits bolt upright.

Tony Mum!?

Something. A hand had held his head.
Let him rest. That feeling.

From the ceiling Tony sees something fall.
A moth. Flutters. Down.
Brushes his arm.

Tony Mum?

Mum wasn't a moth.
He was going soft. No sleep.

The moth flies up to the altar and then . . .
There.
In the corner. Sitting on a ledge high up in the dark.

A statue of Mary. Her bleeding heart.
Something about the eyes, he knew. If his mum's was
    number one, then this was number two.

Drawn toward it, he can't reach.
The pulpit then . . .

He leans. Still can't reach.

And like he was a kid again.
He counts down from ten and on the final 'go' he
    launches himself at the ledge.
Catches it. The statue grabbed and he's on the ground.
And yes the adrenaline kick. The church gloom.
It feels a bit like the Temple of Doom.
Looks at the statue, if what he thinks is true . . .
What would Indiana Jones do?
Of course! He throws the statue to the floor.

   The statue smashes.

And that's when he sees someone at the door.
Staring at him. Horrified.

Tony Hi, Pat. Nice day.

   He suddenly drops to the floor.

He's on the floor and feeling through the smashed bits
    of the Madonna.
Then accidentally sneezes and there's bits of Polo on her.

Pat Tony? Is that you?

Ah! There. Holy moly, he had it in his hand. Bolt upright
    Tony stands.

Tony Yes. It's me.
I was just . . .

Pat Tony. What happened?

Tony I'm afraid there's been an accident.

Pat It didn't look like an accident to me.
Are you having a breakdown, Tony? Is that what this is?
With your mum and . . .

Tony No.
I mean maybe. Yes. Maybe that's what it is.
I'm having a breakdown, Pat, and I'm going to go home
   now.
And deal with it.

Pat Well, can I do anything to help?

Tony I think I just need to be by myself.

Pat Right. Okay.
Only, I will have to say.
About the statue.
I can't lie.

Tony Yes, Pat. I understand. Goodbye.

Go. Go.
Round the corner he stops. Finds a nook.
Unrolls the scroll. Takes a look.

Tony Dear God. I'm sorry I never believed in you before.

And with that he's lost to the parchment in his lap.
   Faded, yes, strange, for sure. But he can see that it's
   a map.

NINE

We see Mikey cycling along.
   We see Gill getting ready for her party.
   *We see Tony studying the map and putting on his
explorer outfit.*

The Roman legions passing by stopped to have an ale
The alehouse went from strength to strength
The Roman horses needed shoes, a blacksmith
    came and opened too
A mobile brothel travelled up from Kent

Oh Little Bevan
So small and yet so fine
Oh Little Bevan
You're growing all that time

The Angles, Saxons and the Jutes, came to Norfolk,
    put down roots
The Vikings came and stirred it up again
The Normans came in sixty-six and added to the
    crazy mix
They all got medieval on the Fens.

Oh Little Bevan
I'd love to settle here
Oh Little Bevan
If property weren't so dear
Too many empty second homes around here.

(Eight hundred thousand for what is basically a
shed. Where were we? Oh yeah!)

Instrumental.

Then the plague came and they all died
Except for a brother and sister survived
They went forth and multiplied
Which is probably why I'm cross-eyed

Then the golden age of steam
A dirty smell came off the stream
And the washing on the washing lines went black
Then the Great War did come

The lads went off to fight the Hun
So many left and so few came back

Oh Little Bevan
Sweet beneath the Norfolk sky
Oh Little Bevan
You fall and then you rise

Well that brings us up to now
Is there anything that we left out?
Anything we left out?!
The General Strike, World War Two
the NHS and Doctor Who
That should do.
Oh!
Thatcher, Major, Tony Blair, Gordon Brown (gosh,
he had flair)

Cameron, Theresa May, Boris Johnson and Brexit . . .
nearly.*

TEN

Gill has finished putting on her Harvest Moon costume.

Gill looks at herself one last time.
The effect was . . . better than she ever could've hoped.
Listens for Rob down below.
This bit was always her favourite. The bit before, when
everything is there. Ready. Gleaming. Not yet spoiled.
Still.
Rob would put a record on. The Moody Blues was the
one she liked.

We hear the song play in the distance.

And together they would have just one glass of wine.
Cold. Fresh. Time together.

---

* This should be altered accordingly.

A finger in the pavlova. A scoop. A treat. Before all those
    feet traipsed through.
Time. Just the two.
Marriage. Mellow.
I have this. I have it.

ELEVEN

Mikey is cycling like mad.

Mikey Shit. Shit.
Come on. Come on.

Ten past nine. Late.
Because of some arsehole reversing out their gate.

AH!

Driver Hey!

Mikey Why don't you watch where you're going?

Driver Why don't you get some lights?

Mikey What do you call this!

Mikey is holding up a tiny light.

Driver A piece of piss.
You shouldn't be on a bike. The countryside is not for
cycling.

Mikey That's my wheel dented.

Driver Well, come on in. I've got the kit.
I'll straighten it.

Mikey Really?

Driver Yes. And here. Have this.

Mikey is given a high-vis vest.

And this.

A massive bike light.

And this.

More high-vis, maybe taped round him with reflective gaffer.

Mikey Really?

Driver Yeah. I bought them for my son. Though he
would never wear them either.
Then some driver killed him.
On the 143.
So, just watch it.

Mikey Right.

Light on tarmac. Nine miles, then ten.
Starts to feel like he's a bubble, floating alone.
The occasional eyes lit, then gone.
Above the sky is this . . . majesty.
Weird tonight. He feels so . . . right. Here. Now.
Then . . . (*Looking at the time on his phone.*) Holy cow!

He pedals even faster.
    Knackered.

There. The Bell.

Mikey Oh God. Oh God oh God oh God.

Dumps his bike.
And it's like he's not really here.
A trance as he goes to the door.
Whoa!
Someone coming out.
Turn about.
No.
No.
No.

He's done three quick turns. Away and back again.

You can do this.

But as he gets to the door. He sees him.
Sitting at the bar.
And . . .

Mikey freezes. Thumps himself, hard. Upset.

Mikey Come on! NO!
You pathetic piece of shit.
No.

Imagination. The killer. Because he imagines the next
    bit. Before it's happened.
And that's the thing. What he always does. Like he
    imagines telling his mum.
And it's there. Again. The slow thing. Rising up.
    This horrible slithering. A snake round his throat.

'You can't do it. You know you can't.'

Stood. Still. His hand on the door.
He sees it fall.
Backs to the side.
And looks through the window.
The boy there.
Looking nervous too.

Mikey I want you.

But all he can do is stare.
Notices his breath in the air.
And thinks. That's me. That breath there.
In. Out.
Clouds.
He'll be dead forever.
Doesn't notice the boy, his date, till he's there.
Come out for some fresh air.
Looks at his phone.

Mikey just stares.
The guy looks at him.

Date Alright?

Mikey nods.

You got a light?

Mikey shakes his head.

Cool.

And then puts his cigarette away.

Mikey wants to say. Wait. Stay!
Please. Hold me.
Something. Something.

But the guy has gone to his car.
The Bell quite far.
To come for a date that doesn't show.
Should've known.
Always the way. Nowadays. No one got any . . .
He seemed nice too. The chat good. *1984*. At his car
    door.
Think we're living it.

NOOOOOOOOOOO!

All of it.
Gone.
Mikey's phone buzzes.
He's actually got reception.
It's a message from the guy.

— *Came. Would've been nice to say hi.*

Pedal.
Pedal.
Who cares.

This place.
This place is dead.
This place is gone.
Just needs to get home.

> *Mikey is pedalling. Distressed. Tears.*
> *Suddenly his bike goes wrong.*
> *He falls.*
> *Still for a second.*
> *Then he's up and kicking at his bike.*

Mikey I hate you.
I hate you.
I hate you.

> *He picks up the bike and throws it in a bush.*
> *He picks up a piece that has fallen off and throws*
> *it away.*
> *Then he runs after it.*
> *Into the darkness.*
> *Into the woods.*

That was Mikey upset.
And if we can't get a real bike then you should know
  that what happened was the wheel fell off. Literally.
And something snapped inside him too.
A little bit of something that had held him all these years.
And through the tears he'd seen the woods outside Little
  Bevan and he'd wanted it. The darkness. The oblivion.
  And he wanted to run through it.
And be torn and dirty and filthy till something else
  snapped.
So he'd run off like that.
All to say, he wasn't having a very good day.

> *We hear Mikey offstage. His fury has driven him wild.*

TWELVE

Nine forty-five.
Ooooooh
Isn't it fun.
All this stuff going on.
A teenage boy on the run.
Gill's party. We'll get to that soon.
And the moon.
Oh la lune!
Gorgeous fecund glowing orb.
Look at her go!
Shining tonight like never before. Bringing madness to
    all below.
The same moon that would've shone when the Vikings
    swarmed this land.
The Heathen Army. Mothers fear. Children's tears. Nuns'
    swarm. And underground. Not a sound.
A saint sleeps on. The peace profound. Waiting for what?
Dot dot dot.

Up above.

*Tony is dressed in his explorer gear. It looks slightly
mad.*

Tony is hunting in the dark.
Trying to pretend he's in *Raiders of the Lost Ark*.
Compass, coat, torch, hat. He'd done a copy of the map.
Blown it up so he could see the faint 'X', marking what?
Could it really be the spot where Agathus was buried.
So much changed in a thousand years, but one thing
    was still clear.
The area known as Nun's Down. Creepy. About a mile
    out of town deep in the ancient woods.
He knew he should wait till morning.
But something had drawn him here. Now.

He'll just have a go.
Be in bed by eleven.
How little he did know.

We see Tony enter the woods.

THIRTEEN

Eleven o'clock.
Gill looks about at what she's created.
The night she's waited for.
The special ingredient she grated into the punch. The
    stew. The cheese fondue.
Was having an effect.
Everyone was well and truly wrecked.

The music explodes.
We see various people from the village dancing.

Josie Gill, this punch it's . . .?

Gill Thanks, Josie.
Won't you have some more?

Josie I'm not sure.
Are my teeth showing?
I think I can taste the moon tonight.
Gosh, I wouldn't normally say that. Would I, Gill?

Gill No.

Josie Still, a little more won't hurt.
It's just so . . .

Gill It's good to let loose.

Josie LOOSE! That's it.

Josie flies away.
Pat arrives.

Pat Gill. Gill.
You'll never guess what –
Oh, I've forgotten.
And it seemed so . . .

She laughs a bit wildly.

Oh Gill. Am I okay?

Gill You're fine, Pat.

Pat Do you have any more of that . . .

Gill Harvest wine?
Of course. Here you go.

They dance. Getting wilder.

Andy Gill!

Gill Andy.

Andy I love your . . .
Well, what are they?

Gill These? These are ears of corn.
Traditionally they were worn –
Oh, but I wouldn't want to bore you.

Josie Gill! You could never bore us.

Josie trying her sincere face.
And so, not without a certain grace, Gill takes to her
    makeshift stage.
And explains what she's wearing. Revenge she'd been
    preparing for six weeks.

Gill You see, I am the Horkey Lord. It's a tradition going
    way back. On Harvest Moon one person in the village
    would be decorated with the fruits of that year's
    harvest. Until night fell and well, the village had to
    swallow it down. Eat what they'd grown. Reap what
    they'd sown.

Only there mustn't be any rot in the harvest. One rotten
    apple can spoil the lot.
And it was the Horkey Lord's job to root out anything
    rotten in the community too.
To sing the life of the village that year.
Its lives. Its secrets. Its lies.
So there was nothing left to fester.

The village spellbound now.
Gill filled with some kind of power.
But also . . . this unease. Was it the trees, creaking in the
    sudden still? It felt like they were being watched.
Spirits old unlocked.
A cloud across the moon. And so began the strangest tune.

GILL'S HARVEST SONG

Here in Little Bevan
We've made our little heaven (so sweet)
And all neglect to mention
The things that aren't quite so neat

But a rot that starts small
It'll spread through us all
Unless we lance it like a boil
Secrets hidden much too long
I'll end them with this song . . .

In winter time we stay at home
In private with our vices
Hang around for long enough
You're sure to glimpse a few surprises
There's Pete in his window sobbing, heaving
Ten cans of Stella help the grieving
'I love you.' Too late. She's six months dead.
He pukes into their empty bed

Look at you
You'd swear that butter wouldn't melt

What? Don't tell me you've never felt like saying
  it all?
Telling all our secrets in the village hall.

Like Mrs Hargreaves' cat. You remember, don't
  you, Pat?
The way she used to kill the little birds you loved
  so much (tweet, tweet, tweet)
But tuna laced with poison? Then wrapped in
  a Tesco bag
Mrs Moggins in a shallow grave beneath the
  rabbit hutch

Springtime when the sap doth rise
Best beware of prying eyes
As Polly steals her wardrobe from Josie's washing
  line
And Steve's screwdriver goes in Andy's brand new
  tyres
In our gentle little village, where do we find the
  time
For dabbling in a delicious little bit of petty crime?

In summer things get hotter still
The truth can be a bitter pill
For those who gamble parish funds
On a losing horse and a few greyhounds
But always hide their tracks somehow
Jan, why not take a bow?
Richard fiddles on his taxes
Mary's son is selling hashish
Pat the klepto steals groceries for kicks
The Motley-Dickson twins are the ones who
    threw the bricks into the hall . . .
So it wasn't 'Gyppo-Davie' after all, though you all
    couldn't wait to call the cops on him
Isn't it a sin
This village we all live in?

And Mrs Hargreaves though you're a thousand
      years old
It's time that everyone was told
Who spread about that nasty cold
That laid the whole village low

Oh Josie, it's you I've saved for last
The thing I saw while walking past
Those plantation shutters you should close
You leave yourself so very exposed
When making the beast with two backs like that
I recognised your meaty thighs
With Steve away I was surprised.
Then! Of course! I couldn't help but laugh
At the rise and fall of Andy's pale white arse
It was like a cosmic thing
A hairy moon round a Saturn ring

O Little Bevan
We've made our little heaven
A bed to lie in, the fruit we've grown
Now let's reap what we have sown

FOURTEEN

Mikey's lit a fire.
And as a ritual sacrifice he's put on it his bike tyre.
It was all there, like it was waiting for him.
Someone else been before and left charred bits of wood
    and a lighter too.
Watches the flames.
Long time.
Sounds of the wood.
He's sat so long he's forgotten who he is.
Which is just perfect.

FIFTEEN

Tony's not sure what he saw.
It was just a feeling.
Like there was someone behind him.

> *Tony jumps.*

Ah!
Then from a tree something flies out and blinds him.
And before he knows, he's stubbed both toes.
And is sort of making a strange sound.

SIXTEEN

The ghost of Nun's Down.

Mikey Who's there?

Synapses flare.
What was he doing all alone out here?

> *Mikey and Tony run around, both terrified.*
> *Then they come face to face and scream.*

SEVENTEEN

Tony Michael?

Mikey Tony.

Tony What are you doing out here?

Had the boy been crying? Streaks of tears.

Tony What's wrong?

Mikey ...
Nothing.

Tony Well, you shouldn't be here.
And you certainly shouldn't be lighting fires at this
   time of year.

And Michael feels this thing.
Like anger inside, growing.
At this man who he'd heard people say.
Was 'a bit funny', 'a bit that way'.
Glasses taped together. Sad and old.
Mikey feels something take hold.

Mikey You know what they say about you, don't
   you, Mr Grieves?

Tony What?

Mikey The village. They say you're weird.
'Poor Tony, all alone with his mum.'
They say it isn't natural for a man of sixty-one.
They say you stare at the kids. Is that true?

Tony What?

Mikey I just wondered what you were doing out in
   the woods at night?
What is it? Some kind of paedo's delight?

Tony Michael!

And right on cue the tape on Tony's glasses goes.
They ping off his nose into the undergrowth below.

   Tony scrabbles to find them. Mikey watches.

This man scrabbling round, was this all there was?
   Mikey feels sick to even be close.
Turns to go home.
Back to it all.

And with that, what can only be described as a crack
   opened up in the earth below.
And little Mikey was swallowed whole.

What?

I know. Dramatic, right? A sort of fight, then this. An almost biblical rending of the earth. Turf thrown high, some going right in Tony's eye.

Tony Ah!

And from far below.

Mikey (*fading*) Oooooooooooh!

Tony Michael!
MICHAEL!

And Tony, not really thinking.
Slides to where Mikey had started sinking.

Tony Hang on, Michael!

The last thing he sees above, the moon's glow.
As he slips, feet first, into the world below.

    Interval.

EIGHTEEN

*Gill is running wildly through the woods. Nettles sting
her legs, brambles whip her. Her clothes are becoming
ripped and torn.*

Gill Come on! COME ON!

Gill can't remember the last time she's been like this.
Heart beating, feet stumbling, brambles ripping her legs.
Completely out of control.
She can hear the rest of the village in the distance.
After her.
For what she's done.
Every secret of the village she'd sung.

The silence right after. When even the night sounds
    seemed to stop.
An owl in a tree. Shocked.
It was Pat what did it.
Though later she said it felt more of a group thing.
A sort of spontaneous rising of shamanic powers.
Blood lust flooding the brain.
And making even the most sensible, practical person,
    someone who, for example, might have read the entire
    North Norfolk Environmental Impact Planning
    Guidance Booklet temporarily INSANE!

Do it.
Do it.
Do it.
Do it.

Some ancient power taking over.
Rising in them all.

Their eyes not quite human.
Gill swore she saw a glint of red pass over Josie's bulging
    orb.
As Andy picked up a rock.

What?

Surely not.

Well, maybe not, but it all got a little heated.
As Gill retreated.
And then, throwing the last of her fruit at the throng,
she'd jumped the fence and run headlong into the woods.

'GET HER!'

And it felt . . . good.
Something. Some kind of something felt good.
Because when was she last in the woods?
Like this. Ripped to bits.
God. When? When did she lose this?

Gill Come on! Come on!

A kid. She'd been a kid.
Something of a memory then flickers through her.
This. This forest all round.
The sound of wind and air and tearing through it all.
She was free once.

Gill I was free!
You hear me. I was free!

Shit.
Her knee goes.
Then she's down.

Gill AH!

  Gill cries out in pain.

The dark above. Canopy.
Her knee. Her bloody knee. She's not a kid.
She's just this thing. This woman. Lying in the dark.

The spark which had lit her.
Suddenly gone.

Gill Help. Help me please.
Someone.

NINETEEN

The tunnels below the woods.
  The distant sound of holy music.
  It's pitch black.
  Tony comes to.
  He crawls.
  He bumps into Mikey, who wakes with a fright.

Tony Michael?

Mikey Yes.

Tony Are you okay?

Mikey I don't know.

Tony Hang on. I just –

  He finds his torch. Turns it on.

There.

Mikey Where are we?

Tony . . .
  The Burrels. They're real.

Mikey What?

Tony Tunnels. Below the woods. They're much deeper
than I thought.

Mikey Right.

Tony No wonder no one's ever found them. No one's
been here for over nine hundred years.

Mikey So . . . we're . . .
Hello?
Hello!

Tony Michael. Are you okay?

Mikey Yeah. I just.
I'm not good in small spaces.
I don't –
Oh God.
Please.
Get me out.
Get me out!

He looks at his phone.

Mikey There's no signal.
There's nothing.

He starts hyperventilating.

Towards the end when Tony's mum wasn't much there.
But sometimes would rise up like she was coming up
    for air.
Seeing where she was and how she was and this was
    the same sound she made.
Losing control.
And so Tony knows.
He knows what to do.

Tony holds Mikey, firm.

Tony It's okay. Breathe, Mum. Just breathe.

Mikey calms a little.

Mikey We need to get out.

Tony Okay. We will. But first. We just need to calm down.

Pause as Mikey calms a little more. Still on edge.

'Under the earth was Agathus laid. Into the tunnels below
did her followers go.'

Mikey What?

Tony It's the only recorded mention of the tunnels.
The *Liber Eliensis*.

. . .

Book One.

. . .

Page 12.

. . .

Paragraph 3.

Mikey What were they for?

Tony To escape. The madness. You see, the Danes had
arrived.

Mikey The Vikings?

Tony . . . Sort of.

'This year eight hundred and sixty-five. The heathens
made great slaughter with the North Folk. And did
burn the corn and sleep with their horses.'

Mikey Don't stop.

Tony What?

Mikey Just keep talking.
I don't care if it's boring.

Tony Thanks.

Mikey Please. It helps.

Tony I can't.
I mean –

  Mikey looks. Waiting.

I'm not very good at . . .

Mikey You're fine.

Tony Okay. Well, once . . .
Once upon a time, I suppose.

Mikey That works.

Tony A terrible curse fell upon the land of the East Angles. That's us.

Mikey I'm not stupid.

Tony The Danes were raping and pillaging the land. But that wasn't all. Crops had failed. The Bishops started to say God had left. And looked about for someone to blame. For years the nuns around Little Bevan had lived quietly. But some said their ways were odd. Against God. Rumours spread that in the dead of night they worshipped the moon. Soon it was decided by the men in Rome they must be disbanded. Their treasures handed over to the Vatican. And that would've been that. Except for one amongst them who said no.

And strangely Tony feels this ease.
For the first time in his life. He stops worrying about getting it all right.
About the details.
He tells Mikey about St Agathus.

> *The story of St Agathus takes over.*
> *In shadow and with music.*
> *We see the Vikings arrive. The land swarmed.*
> *The Pope in Rome turn his back.*
> *St Agathus herself with her sword.*
> *Her escape. Into the woods.*
> *And then her disappearance into the earth below.*
> *It's really beautiful. It comes to an end. They are*
> *alone again.*

Mikey That was good.

Tony Well, it was a very truncated version. Almost embarrassingly simplistic. I mean, to have any real sense of –
. . .

Thanks.
Better?

Mikey Yeah.

Tony Come on then.

The two move off.

TWENTY

Josie Gill?

Pat.

And with that the others arrive.

Sweat.
Heave.
Breath.
Breathe.

They'd actually enjoyed it.
This run through the night.
The hunt. Tails wagging. Eyes bright.

Formed a pack.
Anything was better than looking back at what had
    been said.

Though Steve had at one point looked at Andy there
    ahead and wanted him dead. Just a push over a rock.
    Something that would shock the bastard who'd slept
    with his wife.
They'd all felt it.
Exposed.
Raw.
Better to run than remember.

But now.
Now they were suddenly still.

Gill. This huddled wretch.

Half-naked. Lying on the ground.

What are they meant to do?

Gill can feel it too.

Something change.
They go from being deranged to what?

Josie is the first to say.

Josie Gill, are you okay?

Gill NO. No.

You won't do this.
Go back to how it was before.

Gill Come on. Do something.

Bring this night to a head.

Gill Do it! I know you all want me dead.

Pat Dead?
What do you mean?

Gill And with that Gill couldn't help but recall.
The summer day that started it all.

TWENTY-ONE

In the tunnels.
  Mikey and Tony come to a dead end.

Mikey What?

Tony It's blocked. Fallen in.

Mikey Are we going to die here?

Tony No. We just need to go back. There'll be a way out.

Mikey Right. Sure.

Do you have anything to eat?
I feel a bit . . .

Tony Polo?

Mikey Do you know what's nice?
The quiet.

They listen.

Tone.
Don't you have a phone?

Tony No.

Mikey What's that like?

Tony I don't know. I just never have. I suppose with
my mum things have rather passed me by.
I did once go on Facebook.
But to be honest it was all rather . . .

Mikey What?

Tony Well, seeing the people from school; partners,
kids. I dunno.
I suppose. It can make you feel lonely.

Mikey Yeah.
. . .
You know I was actually on a date tonight.

Tony Oh right. Good?

Mikey I stood him up.

Tony I see.

Mikey Oh. Him. I said him.
I've never said that before.
I've always thought . . .
Well. It just came out.

Tony Maybe it's the effect of being deep underground.
The Agathus effect.

Mikey Yeah!
Sorry. Only . . .

He is crying, suddenly overwhelmed.

Tony That's okay.

Mikey I wanted to tell my mum.
But it's like there's this thing inside. And whenever I try
    I just . . .
It chokes me up.

Tony I used to get that. Lecturing. Even when no one
    came.
A sort of tightening up?

Mikey Yeah.
I mean, it's happening a bit now.

Tony Maybe you just need to practise.

Mikey What?

Tony Well, saying it out loud.

Mikey Right.

Tony Go on then.

Mikey What? To you?

Tony Unless . . .
Yes.

Mikey What do I say?

Tony . . .
I'm gay?

Mikey Me too!

Tony No. No. I was being you.

Mikey Oh right.
. . .
I'm gay.

Tony Mum.

Mikey Mum, I'm gay.

Tony That's it. Sounds good.

Mikey Mum, I'm gay.

. . .

I'm a big gay goose.

Tony I'm as gay as you like.

Mikey I'm a goosey gay gander.

Tony Like a lovely old mop.

Mikey Like the top of a tree, waving in the wind.
    Somewhere on a mountainside.
That's me, Mum.
That's me inside.

. . .

She'll be alright.

Tony Of course she will.

Mikey I liked your mum.
She was fun.

Tony Was she?

Mikey She used to let me play with her fridge magnets
    when I was little.

Tony Oh, yeah. The strawberry and that big shoe.

Mikey She had all the alphabet too.

Tony Really? She must've got that for you.
Wasn't there when I was a kid.

Mikey I sometimes hid in her kitchen. Spelled out rude
    words.
Your mum would do them too.

Tony Mum? No.

Mikey Had a filthy mouth on her.

Tony She was always so strict with me.

Mikey People change when they get old.

He hears something, calming and peaceful and far away.

What's that?

Tony can't hear anything.

Tony What?

Mikey That song. It's beautiful.

Mikey is getting woozy.

I like you, Tony.
Glad you're here.
Sorry I called you a paedo.
Feel a bit . . . weird . . . though . . .

Mikey faints. Tony catches him.

Tony Michael?
Mikey!

TWENTY-TWO

That day.
She'd got back to find Rob gone.
Just a note. After thirty-three years.

'Don't know what to say. I've tried. But you're always too busy. Or just don't want to listen. I hope we can still be friends. The end. Rob.'

Didn't know what to do.
Then realised she was late.
It was the day of the summer fete.
Gill had organised almost everything. Marquees, floats, face-painting.

She'd got Jan to redesign the coconut shy. Because people were always asking why there couldn't be a bit more glitz.
Told them to stick bits of the Christmas panto set here and there.
Now you could throw a coconut at an elf, a reindeer or a life-size cut-out of Cher.

Hello?
How are you?
Lovely day.
Aren't we lucky it turned out this way?

And indeed it had been nice.
Gill felt like maybe it would be okay. Maybe she could say to Pat, or Jan later on. Coming back to find him gone. Rob.

But not now. Now was the time they all loved most.
The dunking of the Dowsy Post.
Every year an effigy was made. Of someone famous who was taken to the river and thrown in.
This year there was a real buzz.
No one knew who the effigy was. That was a secret and the highest bidder got to choose. Raise money for the new roof.

The crowd all round.
The Dowsy brought out. Covered in a sheet and twenty foot tall.
Gill loved this bit.
Though over by the wall she thought she saw Josie, a slight snicker.
Was it?
And almost before it happens. Gill feels this sort of sickening inside.
Jan pulls on a rope and the sheet comes off.
A breath. The whole village looking at this thing.
'Is it Theresa May?' says someone from out of town.

But everyone knows, hands down.
Who it is.

Smile. Smile. But inside Gill is dying.
She can't stop now. She can't start crying.
The village a bit . . . awkward really, but then someone
  screams the Dowsy Song.

Gill walks along.
A hardening inside.
This is what she'll do.
Just watch.
As she's taken to the river.
Her legs set on fire.
Then thrown in.
And no one says.
Are you okay?

Gill Not one of you said a thing.
You all just watched or joined in.
Throwing stones at me.
How do you think that feels?
To see your head stoved in with a rock.

The shock of seeing yourself half sinking.
Bedraggled, submerged and thinking as you float away.

Gill This is me. I am that.

Pat Oh Gill.

Pat the first to speak.

Pat I'm sorry.
I knew it wasn't right. But I just . . .

Gill Let it go. I know.
Do you really hate me so much?

Pat No.

Gill Then why?

And though Pat would never normally want to cause
   a fuss.
She thinks maybe this is what we're here for. Brought
   here. Us.
And so she says.

Pat I think because you sometimes make people feel . . .
   well, like they can't do anything right, or that they're
   not good as you.

Gill What?
Is this true?

Everyone nodding.

Gill I didn't know.

TWENTY-THREE

Tony is carrying Michael through the tunnels.
   It's hard. Really hard. Tony falls.

What do you do?
With a boy of fifteen that has no one else. No one to help.
You look at him and you say.

Tony We are not giving up. No way.

You lift and heave and get to your knees.
You will manage this.
Get to your feet.
Carry him.

Voices Tony. Tony.

You're going crazy. Tunnel upon tunnel of black.
But you swear you can hear this . . .
Tap tap tap tap.

Tony Hello? Hello?
Help.
Please!

TWENTY-FOUR

Gill But I just . . .

I want the village to be good. To be a place where people
 can feel . . .

Like we did.

Do you remember when we first moved here, Pat? Me
 and Rob.

Pat Yes.

Gill You made us feel so welcome.

And it was like there was always something on.

Wasn't there always something on? I feel like the hall
 was never empty. And there were kids in the village.

Where have they all gone?

I think there's a couple of them at Number 21 by Peter's.

Gill But we never see them.

Remember when you could afford to have a family here?

Before second homes left empty all year

And the New Year's Party. What happened to that?

Where everyone had to design their own hat.

Andy, you did that lovely one with the 'Twelve Days of
Christmas'.

Andy Oh yes. 'Seven swans a-swimming.'

Pat 'Six geese a-laying.'

They all sing.

'Five gold rings.'

Gill You see I just want it to be like it used to be.

A place to feel at home. A place for us. All of us. Well,
 just as long as you join in. Come to even just one
 thing. Christmas carols, or the Easter fete. Just make
 a bonnet for God's sake.

Do the flowers.
Give a couple of hours.
To this village.
To this village and it will pay you back so very much
    more.
Just make a jam.
Wash some cups.
Check up on some of the older folks.
Who can't get around.
Or have an idea.
We'll all muck in.
A cheese-rolling competition.
A pasta night.
Dress as druids for the midsummer light.
A day out.
A day out. Even that would do.
A walk round the village.
A pint or two.
Something to bring us together.
Was all I wanted.

Josie Gill. We all want that.

Gill Do you?
But no one ever seems to help.
Sometimes I feel like I'm dragging you all along.

Josie It's because you never let us do anything.

Gill Because no one else ever does it . . .

She's about to say 'right'. But she stops herself.
Not tonight.

Then she looks at her neighbours, the people she's lived
    with so long. Shuffling. Unsure.
Sees the hurt in Josie's eyes.
Notices Steve there too.
Can barely look at the woman he thought he knew.
It floods in on Gill, just what she's done.

Gill I'm sorry, everyone.
I'm so sorry.

And something. Yeah. Maybe just a little something
    starts to lift.
Shift.
Not it all.
But maybe they could deal with the fallout tomorrow.
And the next day. And the next five hundred after that.
For now they pick up Gill.

Are you okay?

Gill Yes.
    (*Realising her costume is torn to bits.*)
Though could anyone lend me a jumper?

TWENTY-FIVE

We have seen Tony struggling through the tunnels.
Dragging Mikey with him.
    He gives up and sits. An exhausted pile.

Tony Help.
HELP!

    His light flickers and goes out.

I'm sorry.
Sorry for it all.

And there in the earth he imagines himself held, protected
    from all the world's torment. From the last six years.
    The bills unpaid, from the need to wake up every day.
    People on the street looking at you with pity; poor
    Tony, he's let himself go. He knows that's what they're
    thinking. He knows when he looks in the mirror that
    what they see is a strange man. Hair long and thinning,

beard needs trimming, his big glasses held on one side
with tape. His clothes a mess, shapeless and old. He
knows. He doesn't need to be told, but inside him is a
heart. Please. He does have a heart. And his mother
was the last to really see it. His mother who he cared
for begrudgingly, but loved so . . . lovingly. A jigsaw
they did, Sunflowers. Sitting in front of the TV for hours.
The sound of her snoring; in, out. The days they
would just drive about, not speaking much, but
knowing a sort of quiet together. 'Oh, they've opened
a new café,' she'd say, and he'd look too and agree.
Peacefully.

All that passes Tony by as he thinks. This is it.

Sees all around him.
A glow.
Is it a glow?

Tony Is this what it feels like to go, Mum?
It's not so bad actually. I hope you felt like this at the end.
I hope you can forgive me.

> *The music of Agathus has risen now.*
> *Agathus has appeared and unbeknownst to Tony*
> *she wakes Mikey up.*
> *He stares at her, then tugs on Tony's sleeve.*
> *Tony looks at the vision before them.*

Tony Yes?

> *She beckons, they follow her. Into the dark. Tony*
> *supporting Mikey.*

Delirious maybe. Strange visions they saw.
The two explorers together.
Following, breathless, the Holy Lady of the Fens.
And then . . .
And then . . .

> *The two have been led into a large, cavernous space.*

An opening-up. A cavern so tall it was lost in the
    darkness above.
And there. In the centre of the space.
Was Agathus' last resting place.

Bones. Just lying, so simple. Small.
Almost like she'd laid down.

'Tony . . .
Love.'

And the sound. That song his mum used to sing.
A beautiful thing.
Tony has tears in his eyes.
And finally. Six months since her death. He cries.

*Agathus' presence fades. But not before she has put
something in Tony's hand.*

And there. A noise.
Close.

*The muffled sound of people singing 'The Twelve
Days of Christmas'.*

Mikey Is that 'The Twelve Days of Christmas'?

Tony Yes.
From where?

Mikey It's coming from the tunnel, over there.

TWENTY-SIX

*The sound of people singing rises until we are with Gill.
    Everyone is singing 'The Twelve Days of Christmas',
but maybe with different words.*

Above something has begun. A sort of village rota.
    Everyone chipping in and Gill has even resisted the

urge to be the one to write it all down (though maybe tomorrow she might just email it round).

Jan I mean, I could take over the tables for art club, if you like

Says Jan.

I never really do much down
    there. I've always felt a little scared to be honest, of stepping on your toes.

Gill No. No. The tables would be wonderful.

Steve I know someone with a marquee for next year's fete. I just always thought I was too late to help.

Says Steve.

Josie takes Gill aside.

Josie Gill, I'm sorry about Rob.

Gill You all knew, didn't you? How long?

Josie Four weeks. He told Steve. We didn't want to intrude and you seemed so determined to . . .
Tell us in your own time.

Gill Yes.
That's actually – Well, it's quite kind.

Mrs Hargreaves If you want, Gill, I'd be very happy to run the raffle on a Thursday.

Gill nods, but makes a mental note to avoid that one, Mrs Hargreaves was known to be a bit scatty. And was better off installed as the chatty one to welcome people at the door.

And soon there's a sort of relaxing in Gill. She can feel herself fill with something . . . what is that?
Is it community spirit?
Feels nice.
To be out.